Kaitlyn Salvatore

IN ASSOCIATION WITH

Published in 2025 by Britannica Educational Publishing (a trademark of Encyclopædia Britannica, Inc.) in association with The Rosen Publishing Group, Inc.
2544 Clinton Street, Buffalo, NY 14224

Copyright © 2025 by Encyclopædia Britannica, Inc. Britannica, Encyclopædia Britannica, and the Thistle logo are registered trademarks Encyclopædia Britannica, Inc. All rights reserved.

Rosen Publishing materials copyright © 2025 The Rosen Publishing Group, Inc. All rights reserved.

Distributed exclusively by Rosen Publishing.
To see additional Britannica Educational Publishing titles, go to rosenpublishing.com.

All rights reserved. No part of this book may be reproduced in any form without permission in writing from the publisher, except by a reviewer.

Editor: Brianna Propis
Book Design: Michael Flynn

Photo Credits: Cover aaltair/Shutterstock.com; (series background) Dai Yim/Shutterstock.com; p. 4 Guido Montaldo/Shutterstock.com; p. 5 Fotokon/Shutterstock.com; p. 6 Andrei Armiagov/Shutterstock.com; p. 7 slowmotiongli/Shutterstock.com; p. 9 (top) Noheaphotos/Shutterstock.com; p. 9 (bottom) Daniel Huebner/Shutterstock.com; p. 10 KT photo/Shutterstock.com; p. 11 aspas/Shutterstock.com; p. 12 Marcos del Mazo/Shutterstock.com; p. 13 Vladimir Wrangel/Shutterstock.com; p. 14 https://commons.wikimedia.org/wiki/File:Etmopterus_perryi_SI_cr.jpg; p. 15 LuckyStep/Shutterstock.com; p. 16 Barou abdennaser/Shutterstock.com; p. 17 Matt9122/Shutterstock.com; p. 18 Luke-diver/Shutterstock.com; p. 19 Pere Grau/Shutterstock.com; p. 21 (top) Wang LiQiang/Shutterstock.com; p. 21 (bottom) Richard Whitcombe/Shutterstock.com; p. 22 FamVeld/Shutterstock.com; p. 23 Nicholas Toh/Shutterstock.com; p. 25 (top) GreenOak/Shutterstock.com; p. 25 (bottom) Rich Carey/Shutterstock.com; p. 26 Jason1214/Shutterstock.com; p. 27 Nataliya Hora/Shutterstock.com; p. 28 Pong471/Shutterstock.com; p. 29 V_E/Shutterstock.com.

Library of Congress Cataloging-in-Publication Data

Names: Salvatore, Kaitlyn, author.
Title: Fish / Kaitlyn Salvatore.
Description: [Buffalo] : Britannica Educational Publishing, [2025] | Series: Discover more: marine wildlife | Includes bibliographical references and index.
Identifiers: LCCN 2024030035 | ISBN 9781641903547 (library binding) | ISBN 9781641903530 (paperback) | ISBN 9781641903554 (ebook)
Subjects: LCSH: Fishes--Juvenile literature.
Classification: LCC QL617.2 .S25 2025 | DDC 597--dc23/eng/20240726
LC record available at https://lccn.loc.gov/2024030035

Manufactured in the United States of America

Some of the images in this book illustrate individuals who are models. The depictions do not imply actual situations or events.

CPSIA Compliance Information: Batch #CWBRIT25. For further information contact Rosen Publishing at 1-800-237-9932.

Contents

A Cool School 4
Underwater Homes 6
How Do Fish Breathe and Swim? 8
Scales and Tails 10
Something Fishy 12
Ancient Creatures 14
Fish Diets 16
From Birth To Death 18
Why Are Fish Important? 20
Swimming in a Tank 22
Fish Threats 24
A Helping Hand 26
Fantastic Family of Fish 28
Glossary 30
For More Information 31
Index 32

A Cool School

Fish are well-known animals that live underwater. Fish come in a variety of shapes, sizes, and colors. One of the smallest fish—the goby—may be less than 0.5 inch (12.7 mm) long. The largest fish—the whale shark—can grow up to 59 feet (18 m) long. Some fish do not have any vibrant, or bright, colors, while others—such as the clown fish and lionfish—have bright colors and patterns on their bodies. Certain kinds of fish resemble, or look like, plants, rocks, or snakes. Others can change their color, and some even glow in the dark.

Many groups of fish, such as tuna, travel in groups called schools of fish. They do this for socialization and safety.

Lungfish are often called living fossils, because their remains have been found to be as old as 380 million years.

Fish live in a wide range of bodies of water, including rivers, lakes, and oceans. They are important in the diets of many people and other animals. Fish are the oldest known **vertebrates**, having lived on Earth for around 530 million years. More than 30,000 species, or types, of fish exist, and new ones are discovered every year.

WORD WISE
VERTEBRATES ARE ANIMALS THAT HAVE A BACKBONE.

Underwater Homes

Fish live all over the world. Most fish are cold blooded, which means they cannot make their own heat. Their bodies are the temperature of the water around them. Some fish live in warm tropical waters, while others live in icy Arctic seas.

Discus fish, which are from the Amazon basin in South America, live in water temperatures of 84 to 86°F (29 to 30°C)!

When salmon are ready to reproduce, or have babies, they swim from the ocean back to the same freshwater river where they were born.

Fish live in all kinds of water. Marine fish live in or near oceans, which have salt water. Freshwater fish live in lakes, rivers, or streams. Some fish, such as certain species of salmon and sturgeon, live most of their lives in salt water but migrate, or travel, to freshwater rivers to reproduce. No fish can live in water that is extremely salty. For instance, the Dead Sea in the Middle East contains so much salt that fish cannot survive there.

Consider This

Fish rely on heat from their environment, or home, to regulate their body temperature. How does this affect what bodies of water they live in?

How Do Fish Breathe and Swim?

Fish do not have lungs like humans—they breathe through structures called gills. The gills allow fish to get oxygen from the water in the same way that lungs help people get oxygen from the air. Some fish also have simple lungs. These fish developed lungs to help them breathe when they have to be out of water for a long time. Walking perch can survive on land for several days when they cross land to move from a pond that is drying up to a fuller pond.

Fish swim mainly by sideways movements of their body and tail. They use their fins to turn, steer, and brake. Some fish shoot a stream of water from their gills, which makes them lunge, or shoot, forward. Flying fish have large fins on their chest. When these fish spring out of the water, they glide through the air with the help of their fins.

As a fish opens its mouth, water runs over the gills and allows oxygen to be absorbed, or taken, into the fish's blood.

compare and contrast

Fish open their mouths to breathe in oxygen from water. Humans suck in oxygen from their noses or mouths to breathe. How are these breathing processes similar? How are they different?

Flying fish can shoot out of the water at 35 miles (56.3 km) per hour or more!

Scales and Tails

Typically, fish have narrow heads and tails with a wider body in between. Nothing sticks out from the body except the fins, which can be pressed flat against the fish. A thin layer of slime also helps fish move quickly through water. A fish's shape is so good at allowing it to move underwater that people design boats and submarines after this shape.

The porcupine fish is covered in spines. When it feels threatened, its spines stand on end to scare away predators.

A shark's scales resemble, or look like, small, bony teeth.

Most fish have scales that overlap each other like shingles on a roof. Fish do not shed their scales like humans shed their hair, but if fish lose a scale, a new one grows to take its place. As the fish grows, the scales also grow by adding rings of new material around the edge. An expert can tell the age of a fish by studying its scales. Unlike people, most fish keep growing as long as they live. Old fish can grow to be very large.

Consider This
How might a fish's shape help it swim underwater?

Something Fishy

Certain fish look strange. They might have unusual shapes and sizes. Seahorses have snouts like a horse and tails that curl around things. Leafy sea dragons are related to seahorses. They look like a leafy plant. Moray eels are long and slender, like snakes. The oarfish has a long, ribbonlike body that can be up to 50 feet (15.2 m) long! A long, red fin runs along the oarfish's back and rises to a high crest on top of the head.

Seahorses are known for not being good swimmers! They only have a tiny fin in the middle of their back to propel, or move, themselves, meaning they swim very slowly.

One type of unusual fish, the electric eel, lives up to its name by creating charges of up to 650 volts with its body!

The Pacific barreleye fish has a see-through head. Frogfish have bumpy bodies that blend into their surroundings of sponges and coral reefs. They use their fins to walk underwater. Some deep-water fish—such as anglerfish and hatchetfish—navigate, or move around, their dark environments with body parts that glow!

Why is the ability to glow helpful for dark-water fish like the anglerfish and hatchetfish? How might their glowing body parts help them catch food?

Ancient Creatures

Sharks are fish with skeletons made of cartilage—a strong connective tissue—instead of bone. Cartilage lets sharks bend and twist. It is lighter than bone, so this helps sharks swim fast. There are more than 400 species of sharks. Most sharks are smart and have well-developed senses. Many sharks can see well even in murky, or cloudy, water, and some sharks can detect, or find, prey using only their sense of smell. Most people are afraid of sharks, but only a few species are known to attack humans. Some sharks—including lemon, mako, and thrasher sharks—are valuable as food.

Dwarf lantern sharks can be smaller than the size of a human hand! Light from their belly helps attract prey and allows them to blend in with sunlight that shines into the dark waters from above.

About 31.2 percent of all shark species are threatened with **extinction**. The biggest threat to these fish is overfishing, or when people take fish at a rate faster than that at which the fish can reproduce.

Sharks are among the oldest types of living things. They live in all the oceans of the world, even in the cold Arctic waters and the seas around Antarctica. The largest is the whale shark. The smallest shark is the dwarf lantern shark. It only grows to about 7.5 inches (19 cm) long.

WORD WISE
EXTINCTION REFERS TO AN ENTIRE SPECIES OF ANIMAL DYING OUT COMPLETELY.

Fish Diets

It is common for almost every fish to eat other fish smaller than them. The smallest fish eat tiny water plants and animals called plankton. Freshwater fish may eat algae, plants, insects, frogs, and other fishes' larvae and eggs.

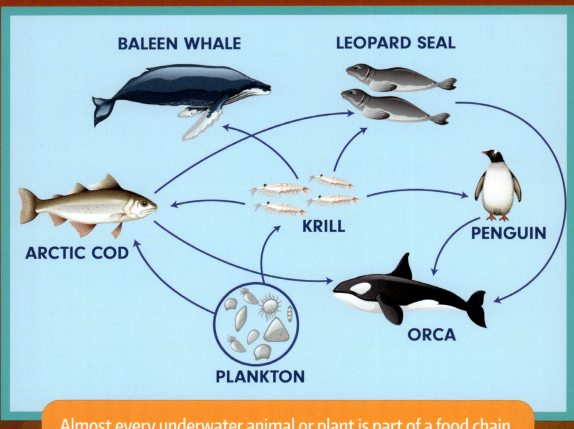

Almost every underwater animal or plant is part of a food chain.

Stingrays and other rays have cartilage instead of bones, like sharks. This allows them to be more flexible.

Sharks are at the top of the food chain in the ocean. Besides fish, some sharks eat seals, dolphins, squid, and even sea turtles. Smaller fish feed on mollusks (including octopuses, clams, and squid), sea stars, and other creatures that live in shallow water or deeper water. Fish that live in the deepest part of the ocean cannot be picky. There is no light or plant life there, so these fish eat other deep-sea animals or whatever scraps sink down to them.

Consider This

Almost every fish in the ocean relies on another fish or animal for food. What happens if one species of fish is overfished? How does human behavior impact the animal food chain?

From Birth to Death

Fish hatch from eggs. Usually, females release eggs into the water and males fertilize them. After a time, larvae hatch from the eggs. Soon, a larva forms a skeleton and develops fins and scales. Many eggs and larvae are eaten by other fish. Some kinds of fish try to protect their eggs by hiding them, but most fish do not protect their eggs or their young.

To increase the chance that some young will survive, a female releases hundreds, thousands, or even millions of eggs at a time.

Most fish eggs are transparent, or see-through. Some people eat fish eggs! Eggs from a fish called the wild sturgeon are called caviar.

A female blue shark usually gives birth to 25 to 50 live pups at a time, but it can be up to 135 pups! Sand tiger sharks, on the other hand, give birth to a maximum of two live pups at once.

Sometimes the eggs are fertilized in the female's body and hatch there. The young are then born live from the female. Guppies, some sharks, and surfperches give birth to live young. A fish **spawns** children of its own after it grows into an adult.

WORD WISE
SPAWN REFERS TO PRODUCING YOUNG, ESPECIALLY MANY AT A TIME. FISH SPAWN BY RELEASING EGGS AND SPERM.

Why Are Fish Important?

Many animals rely on fish for food. Bears, seals, and many birds consume fish as part of their diet. Fish are also an important source of food for humans. People all over the world eat many different kinds of fish, including cod, herring, and tuna.

Fish are also an important part of many ecosystems. Goby fish eat seaweeds that would kill coral reefs. Fish help control diseases such as malaria, yellow fever, and the Zika virus by eating mosquito larvae. And through their waste products, fish provide nutrients that help plants grow. All these things help keep ecosystems in balance. Researchers even use fish in medical studies to find ways to treat or cure skin cancer, heart disease, and muscular dystrophy.

Many bears eat salmon. Many people do too!

compare and contrast

Fish are important to people, animals, and the environment. In what ways are they needed similarly by the three? In what ways does their use differ?

Clown fish live in sea anemones. In exchange for using them as their homes and for protection, clown fish keep the sea anemones clean!

Swimming in a Tank

Fish are one of the most popular pets that people keep in their homes! Goldfish, guppies, and bettas are easy to care for and fun to watch. Koi, a type of carp, come in many beautiful colors and are often kept in ponds in backyards or in parks. Many people set up an aquarium, a special glass tank, which can hold several types of fish. Home aquariums may hold as little as 1 gallon (3.8 L) of water or more than 100 gallons (3,785 L)!

This aquarium has a tank that lets the fish swim over visitors' heads!

Some people with fish tanks have certain snails and plants living in them to help clean the tank! For example, ramshorn snails will clean an aquarium by eating any algae, fish food, or dying plant leaves they find.

Large public aquariums help people learn about fish and their habitats. Most aquariums have many kinds of fish from different parts of the world. Some have underwater tunnels that let people see fish swim around and above them. Some aquariums even have tide pool exhibits or small tanks that let visitors touch certain types of fish such as stingrays.

Consider This
How might aquariums help people to learn about and appreciate fish?

Fish Threats

Fish populations can suffer damage from human activity. When people build dams on rivers, it lowers the flow of water in the rivers. That may prevent fish from swimming upstream to spawn. People also fill in wetlands to make room for buildings. Sometimes people release fish into areas where that type of fish has never lived before. If the fish have no natural enemies in their new habitat, they can quickly multiply and may wipe out fish that were already living there.

People dump garbage and sewage into creeks, rivers, ponds, lakes, and oceans. Factories or cities sometimes release harmful chemicals, oil, and other waste into water. These can poison the fish that live in the water. Global warming is increasing the temperature of Earth's water. The warmer water kills some plants and other things that fish eat. Another problem is overfishing. When people catch too many fish of the same species, that species becomes at risk of extinction.

Oil spills kill many fish and other sea life. Oil spills can happen when a ship is refueled, pipelines break, large oil tanks sink, or drilling operations fail.

compare and contrast

What threats to fish are caused by people? Which are caused by nature? Is one more harmful than the other?

Plastic bags, broken bottles, food wrappers, and cigarette butts are forms of litter that kill fish and harm their food supply.

A Helping Hand

Although there are many threats to fish, we can each lend a helping hand to ensure their protection and the safety of their environments. We can help fish by not building new dams and by removing dams that are no longer needed. In some areas, people have built fish ladders to help fish move past dams so they can spawn. Protecting wetlands also helps protect fish. Many people work to prevent others from accidentally introducing fish into areas where the fish do not belong.

> With a dam, a waterfall, or another form of blockage in the way, fish such as salmon wouldn't be able to swim to their spawning grounds. Thanks to **fish ladders**, they can!

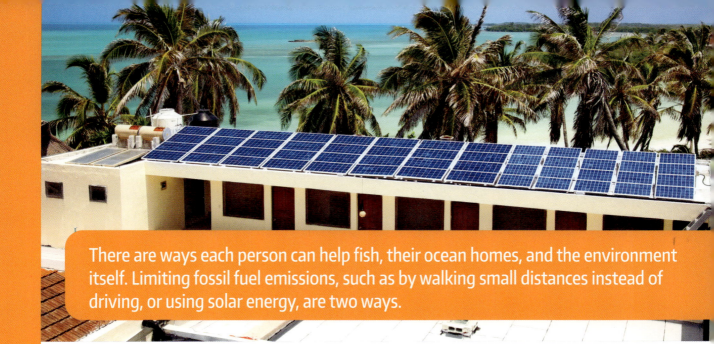

There are ways each person can help fish, their ocean homes, and the environment itself. Limiting fossil fuel emissions, such as by walking small distances instead of driving, or using solar energy, are two ways.

Fish farming helps prevent overfishing of some species. Some types of fish, such as trout, can be easily bred in captivity. Once hatched, they are raised in tanks or ponds. The grown fish are then sold for food.

Preventing oil spills and other forms of pollution will help keep ocean fish healthy. Some countries are working to stop global warming by preventing rivers and oceans from becoming too warm for fish.

WORD WISE
FISH LADDERS, ALSO KNOWN AS FISHWAYS, ARE A SERIES OF ASCENDING—OR GRADUALLY RAISED—POOLS THAT FISH CAN SWIM UP. THEY LOOK LIKE STAIRS!

Fantastic Family of Fish

Even though fish are the oldest vertebrates in the world, people still study, or learn about, them often. People still find new fish species every year. Some fish, like the lionfish, are pretty and colorful. Others, such as piranhas and anglerfish, are creepy and scary looking. Fish live in fresh water and salt water, streams and oceans, and even in dark underground caves. Their homes can be sunny or in the deepest part of the ocean where light never reaches.

A lionfish gets its name because it has flowing spines and fins that look like a lion's mane!

Big or small, fish from every underwater world need our protection!

Some fish live in schools with other fish for protection and community. Other fish, like the moray eel, prefer to live by themselves. Regardless of what a fish looks like or where a fish lives, they are an important group of animals on Earth that need our protection.

Consider This

Different species of fish have various needs, diets, and underwater homes. What are some things you can do to help protect all fish, regardless of their different needs?

Glossary

aquarium A glass tank in which living water animals or plants are kept.
cold blooded Having a body temperature that is not regulated by the body.
ecosystem A community of living things interacting with their environment.
fertilize To join the necessary reproductive parts (e.g. a sperm unites with an egg) in order to create life; to increase the likelihood of reproduction or growth.
global warming A warming of Earth's atmosphere and oceans.
larva A young form of an animal that looks very different from its parents.
malaria An illness that is passed on to humans by the bite of mosquitoes.
migrate To move from one place or region to another.
muscular dystrophy An inherited disease that causes increasing weakness of muscles.
plankton Small plants and animals that float or drift in a body of water.
predator An animal that lives by killing and eating other animals.
reproduce To make new organisms through fertilization, development, and giving birth.
sea anemone A boneless sea animal that looks like a flower and has brightly colored tentacles.
species A group of organisms that have common features and can reproduce young of the same kind.
sperm The male reproductive cell that unites with a female's egg to reproduce.
tropical Having to do with an area that is very warm and wet or humid.
wetland Areas of land, such as marshes and swamps, that hold a lot of water.

For More Information

Books

Caprioli, Claire. *Fish*. New York, NY: Children's Press, an imprint of Scholastic Inc., 2024.

Maloney, Breanna. *Fish*. New York, NY: Children's Press, an imprint of Scholastic Inc., 2023.

Parker, Steve. *Fish*. New York, NY: DK Publishing, 2022.

Websites

Britannica Kids: Fish
kids.britannica.com/kids/article/fish/353130
Discover more about the world of fish, such as their behaviors and reproduction.

Climate Change and Fishing
www.msc.org/what-we-are-doing/oceans-at-risk/climate-change-and-fishing
Learn about how global warming affects fish and fishing.

National Geographic Kids: Fish
kids.nationalgeographic.com/animals/fish
Read more about different kinds of fish from all over the world!

Publisher's note to educators and parents: Our editors have carefully reviewed these websites to ensure that they are suitable for students. Many websites change frequently, however, and we cannot guarantee that a site's future contents will continue to meet our high standards of quality and educational value. Be advised that students should be closely supervised whenever they access the internet.

Index

A
anglerfish, 13, 28

C
clown fish, 4, 21

E
eels, 12, 13, 29
eggs, 16, 18, 19

F
fins, 8, 10, 12, 13, 18, 28
flying fish, 8, 9

G
gills, 8, 9
goby, 4, 20

L
leafy sea dragons, 12
lionfish, 4, 28

O
oarfish, 12

P
pets, 22, 23

S
salmon, 7, 21, 26
scales, 11, 18
seahorses, 12
sharks, 4, 11, 14, 15, 17, 19
skeleton, 14, 18
stingrays, 17, 23
sturgeon, 7, 18

T
tail, 8, 10, 12
tuna, 4, 20